BLUE ELECTRODE

Poems by

Margaret Barbour Gilbert

Finishing Line Press
Georgetown, Kentucky

BLUE ELECTRODE

*for Willie, Aurora Leigh, and Figaro
eternal stars in the night*

Copyright © 2021 by Margaret Barbour Gilbert
ISBN 978-1-64662-540-6 First Edition
All rights reserved under International and Pan-American Copyright Conventions. No part of this book may be reproduced in any manner whatsoever without written permission from the publisher, except in the case of brief quotations embodied in critical articles and reviews.

ACKNOWLEDGMENTS

Carnegie Mellon Magazine: "Aura"
Home Planet News: "Blue Electrode"
Mudfish: "Green Silk Cigar Case," "Seizure," "Fontana di Trevi," "Bell Jar"
Crazyhorse: "Morning Episode," "Morning Come," "Little Sickness,"
"Eating A Piece of Black Bottom Pie With Mother," from *Recapturing Anna Karenina*, "This Is a Photograph of Me, "Picture of Me Having A Seizure," "EEG With Brandy Alexander"
The Examined Life Journal at University of Missouri: "Kindling"
Skid Row Penthouse: "To Phoenicia," "Father Goes To Get The Medicine"
The Tribecca Poetry Review: "Recovery"

Publisher: Leah Huete de Maines
Editor: Christen Kincaid
Cover Art: Ludwig Kirchner, 1912, *Woman at the Mirror*
Author Photo: Stephanie Dickinson
Cover Design: Elizabeth Maines McCleavy

Order online: www.finishinglinepress.com
also available on amazon.com

Author inquiries and mail orders:
Finishing Line Press
PO Box 1626
Georgetown, Kentucky 40324
USA

Table of Contents

Outside My Window ix

Gorgon 1

Aura 2

Green Silk Cigar Case 3

Blue Electrode 4

Kindling 5

This Is A Photograph of Me 6

Morning Episode 7

Morning Come 8

Little Sickness 9

Eating a Piece of Black Bottom Pie With Mother 10

From *Recapturing Anna Karenina* 13

Picture of Me Having A Seizure 23

Fontana di Trevi 24

EEG With Brandy Alexander 26

Seizure 27

Recovery 28

Bell Jar 29

To Phoenicia 30

From *Recapturing Anna Karenina*

OUTSIDE MY WINDOW

I can hear Father's and Mrs. Walker's
voices from beneath the trees outside,
my window, as they discuss Pound, *old men's voices,*
beneath the columns of false marble, the
modish and darkish walls, discreeter
gilding, and the panelled wood suggested,
for this household is touched with an
imprecision, *the house too thick, the*
paintings a shade too oiled. A shadow
moves before me, and the voices lift,
weaving an endless sentence, and their
passion endures, *knocking at empty rooms,*
seeking for buried beauty. I lie heavy
in my arms, dead weight drowning with tears,
thinking of Anna, her gold silk dress
trimmed in velvet, staring at the
brown/yellow wood and the no-colour
plaster. I am the darker sister. They send
me to eat in the kitchen when company
comes. For so long I've eaten the scraps
from the table and licked the crumbs
from the floor. But tomorrow I'll be at
the table. They'll see how beautiful I am
and be ashamed.

GORGON

I am one of those,
unstable as water
with wings and snaky hair,

whose look turns men to stone.
Woman, island, I live alone.
Phorcys, son of sea and earth,

was my father, my mother,
Ceto, a sea monster.
In the mirror of a bright shield,

you can see me clearly,
a dragon-like creature
covered in golden scales

for I was born royal
with snakes for hair
and glaring eyes.

Perseus struck my head clean
from the collar bone.
(I could not turn him to stone.)

Pegasus, winged horse of the gods,
sprang from my Gorgon's blood,
beneath my black hood;

as Perseus stuck his knife
down my throat (the vomit purple
spew), my wings grey heavy,

damp with salt-spray too,
and mindful of the snake-haired head,
he set it down among sweet fern
  and seaweed.

AURA

I felt like angels
were holding me up
when I woke this
morning. I could
see the grey sky
through the green trees
of my window pane,
the clear blue day,
the bright black

hair of angels.
It was as if
I were high above
the earth,
suspended,
riding
an angel's wing
into the mirror
of my life.

GREEN SILK CIGAR CASE

Like the Vicomte in Madame Bovary, you left
your green silk cigar case on the table of the
cafe where we met, and like Emma, I kept it, I
took it to smell your fragrance, to be reminded
of you, who had left for Paris. I

imagine you there in the theaters
and bars with other women. You don't write.

I want to enter you, your life, to be part of
you, just as I opened the case with its green
silk border and found the cigars.

BLUE ELECTRODE

1.
At the moment I am all wired up and
buckled into a $9,000 belt with tape recorder
—getting a 24-hour recording of my brain.
Like Medusa or one of the
Gorgon Ladies, I have over 100 tiny blue
electrodes all over my scalp, wires coming
out of my head and a collar of blue
electrodes around my neck. Paste like clam
dip is smeared through my hair, so
the electrodes will stay in place. I am
planning to call my mother later to see
if she triggers off Seizure Activity.

2.
Among plastic flowers
and eisinglass curtains,
a china chest,
she comes bearing gifts
to the glassed-in receptacle,
a visitor to a grave site,
and mourns the seizures
dressed in black.
Yes, my mother thinks to herself,
 tying her torn scarf,
the words Epilepsy and Woe
are synonymous.

3.
I tie a blue scarf over my head,
so that no one will see the thousands
of tiny wires attached to my skull,
my hair, a mass of twisting snakes,
if I later go out to the grocery.
This is the blue scarf my father
had wanted me to give my mother—
a pale blue the predominant color
with tiny yellow flowers—
I mailed the scarf to her,
but she returned it.

KINDLING

The twigs and branches must be small enough
to fit inside the gold-plated glass doors to make a good fire.
In epilepsy, there's a process called *kindling*

when the neurons in the brain
rub together creating a fire in the head.
The stove is spinning straw to gold

like the Miller's daughter in *Rumpelstiltskin*,
devouring my brain in an epileptic fire.
It casts a spell like Rumpelstiltskin's dance:

Today I'll brew, tomorrow I'll bake.
Soon I'll have the Queen's namesake!

THIS IS A PHOTOGRAPH OF ME

at age thirteen.
At first it seems to be
a smeared print: faded blue tones
blended with the paper.
(It is hard to make me out.)

Then, as you scan it,
you see part of a tree
in the left-hand corner,
and down a gentle slope,
a small white frame house
  coffin-like.

On the edge, there is a bungalow,
where I spent the night
at my neighbor's the summer that
we moved into this house.
Her bedroom had bright pink walls.

I am in the house, in the *center*
of the picture, on my back
in the hallway.
(This photograph was taken
the day after I died.)

My blond hair is pulled
back from the forehead
and curled at the sides in a page boy.
I am wearing a dark
navy cotton blouse.

I have just fallen from the white
vanity bench before my typewriter
in my (blue) bedroom onto the floor.
There is blood at my mouth.
I have wet my pants.

(My parents are at church.)

MORNING EPISODE

Sunlight strikes a glass
Of grapefruit juice
Through green leaves
In the dark forest

Of this very white house.
The pictures on the walls may
Crumble and fall—
Grandmother's pink in Pepto-Bismol.

A pale beige, the walls,
Are silk upon the table.
Suddenly I rise,
Nod awkwardly without looking,

Stumble out of the kitchen
Into the tiny dark hallway.
"What's the matter?"
Calls Mother.

"Can't you even answer?"
I am lost in blackness,
Lost in rooms of green
Furniture.

Like Dante
I'm in a fright
I will not find my way out
Of this dark wood.

MORNING COME

For hours I would lie in the big bed
which fronted the balcony off St. Ann
Street and come.

I lay beneath the tiny garret of
my attic apartment and listened
to the rain on the tiny roof
falling into the street.

I just sat there
on the edge of the bed
and shook like the wind shakes a fruit tree
causing the leaves to scatter and fall to
the ground.

LITTLE SICKNESS

A letter from my mother:
"I feel sure that, as a child, you had
Petit Mal. You looked and sounded as if
you were day dreaming, and you did not
respond or hear or react when we
talked to you. The absences were fleeting
at first. Dr. Little prescribed *tridione*,
(I believe)—and the medicine corrected
the absences for years. When they started
to recur, he changed your medicine. I
do know that he tried several different
medicines—*mebarol* (I think) among
them, and, (I think), *milontin*. I cannot
remember whether he added these to *tridione*
or just eliminated *tridione* for a while.
At any rate, he did not prescribe *dilantin*
until you had the grand mal seizure when
you were in high school. In reading about
complex-partial seizures, I do not remember
any pattern of repetitious, automatic,
purposeless behavior. But you did look
dazed. Since your doctors disagree
in the diagnosis of the the type of epilepsy,
perhaps you have developed another type
of seizure. When I would see your eyes
go "dreamy" or when I would talk to you
and you did not respond, I would call your
name—and in a moment or so, you would
be "back". And you had no consciousness
of your absence. Staring and dreaming
spells?? Yes, you had these."

EATING A PIECE OF BLACK BOTTOM PIE
AT WEIDMANN'S RESTAURANT WITH MOTHER

The pie glitters like a black jade
tiara with little gold lights
in the fudge, topped with a fine white
cloud of whipping cream.
Mother whips me with her tongue:

>*21 large marshmallows,*
>*1 cup of Evaporated Milk.*

Gone is the easy rapport between us.
We sat in the wrong place at the wrong time.
Mother wanted to sit in the center.
I wanted to sit on the side.
Each slice or spoonful,

>*1/2 pint of whipping cream.*

"The center is really nicer,"
said Mother.
"There are too many people in
the center," I said.
(Why do we always have to argue?)

>*1/2 cup of melted butter or margarine,*
>*4 tablespoons of Bourbon.*

This should be a happy time.
But Mother refuses to order.
"I'll just have a small Spinach Salad
and Black Coffee."
I've ordered Black Bottom Pie.

"You don't need a piece of
Black Bottom Pie," said Mother.
Her eyes twinkle like the little
beads of sweat

that sparkle on the black icing.
I decide to take my time eating it,
if it ever comes.
"I rarely come in here
anymore because the colored help is
so slow," said Mother.

> *1 box of Nabisco Chocolate Snaps*
> *to line the bottom.*

"This corner is like an oven!
She offered us the best place
and you refused it.
I like to sit in the center,"
said Mother, "Whew!"

> *Melt marshmallows in hot milk,*
> *(do not boil!) fold whipped*
> *cream into marshmallow mixture.*
> *Add bourbon and pour into cooled*
> *chocolate crust.*

We have been shopping.
I love the gold suit of raw silk
and the black leather pumps.
But I'm unsure about the blue skirt.

"Most people just take a little of that
blue cheese dressing—Not guzzle it
down, like you do."

"It's so good. I don't come here often,
you know."

"I know. But those people at the next
table are looking at you."

Bake in 350 degree oven until crust has set. Cool. Top with whipped cream and bitter grated chocolate.

from RECAPTURING ANNA KARENINA

I
Inside the bedroom with its close sweet-smelling
  Air and roses of dark gloom, Grandmother
Is in bed. She has a glass of milk and a plate
  Of crackers on the small stand beside the bed.
The afternoon light against the shades gives this

  Room a dark shadowy bluish glow. It has
The smell of death and roses, the sick sweet
  Smell of heliotrope and heat, wet camphor
"Dear Grandmother," I venture. "I really
  Want to ask something of you. I met

The most wonderful girl in London, and she
  Has invited me to come home with her from
The school and spend two glorious weeks in
  New York City at her home with every type
Of advantage free." In the thick silence I

  Pause. "What do you want to go to New York for?"
Says Grandmother, feebly throwing her hand.
  What I really feel, I say, is that if
I don't get away I will die and the fact
  Of there being very little money now

Because of the epilepsy and my wanting to
  Leave. "But the gaps," says Father helplessly,
Coming to the door. "What gaps?" I say. Father
Says, "The slight gaps like the quivering of a
  Light bulb." "I didn't notice anything," says Mother.

"But there's nothing wrong with me!!" I cry.
  "The little gaps occurring infrequently,"
Father repeats, "like the blinking of a light bulb.
  A light-bulb about to go out—"
"I have no more money, Peggy," Grandmother says.

"And what will I do now? I SAY. "Where will I
   Go?" ------------------------------------
   I stand in the hallway, an unfinished painting
In the deathlike silence of the college buildings,
   My dress, long, white, and torn. I have a cut

   Above my left eye from the seizure, my unfinished
Left eye.
   Mrs. Walker parks her car and gets out. She makes
Her way up the walk. Little stones crunch
   Beneath her purple feet. She hesitates at

The foot of the steps, then crosses the porch
   Very quickly and peers through the gray
Screen door into the dark interior. She
   Carries an armful of books. "Is anybody
There??" she calls through the door, the

   Silence causing her to frown and crunch
A stone beneath her purple toe.
   Through the door: a leg in a rotted fume
   Of stocking and a high-heeled shoe.
Mother is cooking a chicken,

   Mythical bird, part beast and fable,
Parts of which lie strewn about the kitchen
   Table, her baking eye a cloud of dust
As her hands flutter in dough, her cold

   Moist eye runs like gravy upon the table,
      Lies among forgotten wishes,
The gloom and doom of dishes. She bends
      Beneath a kitchen sink, and nothing
Is what it seems. She remembers her

   Lost dreams. Father stands at the kitchen
Sink with a letter. "They don't want you to

Return in the fall," he says, "because
You had that seizure, you know, in the theatre
In front of all those people."

In the kitchen Mother begins to weep,
  Her false charm forsaking all its poses
(And Father wears his brown suit cheap),
  While Mothers cries and then composes
Herself. I can see Grandmother's dark

  Brown hairnets number three thirty nine,
And a square box of Russell Stover candies
  With brunettes on the paper, women with
Deep brown locks, they lie against the dirty
  Lace *magna vox,*

Atop the bureau like fickle courtesans
In velvet rooms afflicted with the pox,
  Dining on soup and cinnamon buns,
But all the women in this house are nuns.
  Grandmother lies in bed as though in mourning,

Her reclining figure draped in blue and burning.
  "You're no queen!" Mother says in deep,
Cutting off the chicken's head. The chicken
  Lies in its skillet bed, where the soup
Purrs bean green on the baking black stove,

In the blue cloud mist of my brain. Far
Off, I hear the train. "No, it wasn't the
  Seizure!" I say. "Why I just have a slight
Headache, that's all!"

The fat crackles in the fire.
The chicken sings. The pan burns.
And the door closes, *Ad Nauseam.*
The kitchen floor rises like a giant wave

A peeling lozenge of bright pink and mauve.
"But where will I go now?" I SAY.
"What will I do?
Footsteps are heard. Grandmother approaches
In the doorway on the right. She
Wears a black dressing gown, and
Clutches a hot water bottle, with slippers
On her feet. The train
Makes a lonely mournful sound.
Mrs. Walker is at the door now.

The brown cloud gloom of the little house
  Is like a coffin. The striking clock, the
Dark hallway, the long mirror.
Dark cramped narrow halls, hung with silver
Mirrors. My mother like a lioness swathed in
  Silk, the sword of her dress piercing me, as
She advances upon me, in that dark narrow hall,
  Dark veils like tiger lilies. My father in
The doorway like an undertaker dressed in black.
  The doorbell rings ... My mother says I am not
At home. A descending candle moves past a window.
  My grandmother is all dressed up with nowhere
To go. She is standing between the bedroom and
  The kitchen in a faded burst of sunlight.
The afternoon light against the pulled shades gives
  The room a dark shadowy bluish glow, moving
Towards me.

"Don't be afraid of me, Peggy," she says, "because
I'm your grandmother—I'm just coming back from
The sanitarium."

A train whistle in the distance. I listen.
The clouds are like roses.

II

I stayed home that summer and lay
   In a dark room for three weeks,
A damp green cloth across my forehead.
   After the large seizure I took one Diamox
      And two Dilantin. I got sick. I tried
Mysoline, then Milontin, and Quinacrine

   —100 mgs. twice daily—,
And *Celontin*. I wouldn't stay on
   The medicine. At nineteen I said
I'm getting old. I used to be

Beautiful before I developed
   Epilepsy and had to take those red
And white pills. I could have been a model.
Now all day long I have been flickering on
   And off like a defective lamp.
The bedroom turns as I study the letter
on a bed covered with blue fabric,
And the fluorescent light winces

   Like a terrible migraine for
The red and white pills that I hate
   And lose and will not take.

Mrs. Walker is at the door.
   "Is anybody there?" she calls
Peering into the darkness out of
   The pouring rain in a very large hat,
   Staring through the screen door.

The doorbell rings again.
"Come in Mrs. Walker," Father says to
Mrs. Walker of Thorn Hill, with its
   Bannisters of heavy solid oak
And four posters slept in by George

Washington and General Robert Lee,
A carved railing set like a crown
Upon its head and plantation bells
   Of black lead.
Mrs. Walker has come by
   With gifts--a still-life pain\ting
Of dark apples on wood, and a box
   Of Russell Stover candies.

There are dark paintings of flowers
   By Mrs. Walker on the walls,
Above the satin couch in the living
   Room, where Mother sleeps,
   Next to a bowl of wax fruit.
   I am in the back bedroom.
I can hear through the thin walls.

Mother says to Mrs. Walker,
   "May I offer you a glass of Iced Tea?"
Mrs. Walker is a mannish woman
In tweeds and high button shoes with iron

   Grey locks of hair cut very short.
Father talks about the book he is writing.
   "You call the South a sick lady?"
Mrs. Walker says. "It seems to me that
   She is," says Father.

Father and Mrs. Walker drink Tokay
In the cold dining room (tomb-like)
And speak about the book he is writing.

Mrs. Walker in a tea-wet voice):
   "It's simply delicious! How elegant
   Your Tokay is!"
There comes a burst of laughter from

The dining room. Father and Mrs.
Walker are enjoying themselves there
  And sex like an autumn fog hangs
Heavy in the air. In the kitchen black
  Inez bends over the stove until
The sweat pours from her back

  Gluing her grey linen dress to her shoulders,
Ballooning it out in places—swelling it
  With hot air. She labors over the ironing

Board; her shoulders are black massive boulders.
  Her thick hands bear down upon
The steaming iron, moving it back
  And forth. Mother is in the kitchen
Cooking lunch. Parts of a cut-up chicken

  Lie strewn about the kitchen table.
Father crosses the room nervously
  with a cigarette, which dangles between
his thin white fingers. They are shaking.
  The college is like a graveyard.

Mother comes into the dining room.
  "And how is Peggy?" Mrs. Walker says.
Mother says: "She's over in London.
  And me—old drab face—I've never been anywhere!"
She laughs nervously. "Yes," says Father.

"She's over in London. Having the time of her life."
I hear my parents say. Lying in the next room,
  I stiffen as they talk about me.
This particular afternoon, Father wears an old
  coat, a crumpled white shirt with shabby tie.

He drinks too much coffee and smokes camels.

"Won't you have a Camel, Mrs. Walker?"
he asks. His green eyes reflect the light.
"No, thank you," says Mrs. Walker, "I don't
 smoke."

"Please have another glass of Tokay,"
Father says. "No," says Mrs. Walker
 "I really can't stay."
I hear Mrs. Walker leave by the front door.
 I can hear her going down the walk.

Father sits in the green wing chair
 In the living room drinking in the dark
Plum-colored interior, reciting
 Shakespeare rose-colored dark.

Pale sunlight on the half-drawn shades
 Reflects my mother's shadow in the kitchen
Bending towards me behind the swinging door,
 "*The epileptic on the bed,*" in the T.S.
Eliot poem.

       III.
Father drove on. The heavy rainfall
Made the dirt road slick in spots and soft.
But he drove on recklessly. His foot was a
Lead weight on the accelerator, and his
Mind filled with thoughts of Mrs. Walker
And his uncompleted book.

Suddenly the car veered off the road, slid
Into a ditch and crashed, or so he said.
He tried to jostle the car loose, but it
Remained firmly implanted in the sticky
Mud,

The rain bombarding the car. He lit a
Cigarette and sat looking out at the
Country dirt road and at the rain on the
Windshield, a cold blue rain.

The Alabama black Belt runs right into the
Mississippi Delta, which ends in New Orleans,
A wild tangled undergrowth of jungle with
Dead black trees and muddy yellow water
Totally cut off from the 20th century.

There were miles of low flat land, broken
Bottles and telephone poles.

He would explain to Mother later that he had
Had a little bit of trouble in the rain coming
Back from Birmingham with the medicine

      IV.
Grandmother in her black hat and traveling clothes
Has just arrived for lunch.

My Grandmother still gleaming like fruit
Is wearing Liz Arden's Blue Grass Perfume
in her black hat and travelling suit.

Father lies on the old green couch in the
dining room because he has a headache.
He stares at the plate of fruit
on the sideboard.

In the light and shadow
 The bananas, an exotic mandrake.
His headache
now making the wall grey, the bananas
  yellow.

He goes down the hall to a back bedroom
 And loads up on whiskey,
A long-barreled blue-back

Revolver against a lace-

Curtained window. His hand wipes
The weapon with a dinner napkin. He
Lays it down by an empty pint whiskey
Bottle on the floor by the bed.

              V.
I spent three months in Rochester, MN
Heavily medicated on *Dilantin*.
First I took 2 *Dilantin* and 1 *Diamox*,
A pill I hated like the Chicken Pox.
Then 3 *Dilantin* and no *Diamox*.
I tried *Mysoline*, *Milontin*, and *Quinacrine*,
 Until my face had turned a Paris Green.
I was saturnine, guillotined, overseen,
Twice daily with *Phenobarital*, Four
Times a day, *Celontin*, and there were visits
From Father. It was so cool up there
Like in the mountains, until the doses
Made me dizzy. Wanting to die,
I came home. My head was in a tizzy.
 But Doctor said my medicine was now
Adjusted.

PICTURE OF ME HAVING A SEIZURE

I am in the Loeb Boat House
seated at a green metal table in a green metal chair
wearing an eyelet dress
by the water (lake)
in Central Park
having two hamburgers and a coke.
I am sixteen and on my first
trip to New York. I am not
having a good time.
My eyes are closed
the look that you see on buses
when a blind person with a dog
and stick gets on and sits in
the front of the bus.

My white envelope bag
lies near the food on the table.

I am not quite all there.

FONTANA DI TREVI

We ate there many times.
It had the feeling of death
about it—a dark Italian
restaurant on West 57th
across the street from
Carnegie Hall.
I am reminded of the smoky corridors
of Dante's Hell by the decor—
smoked silver mirrors,
the gargoyles of
stucco that lined the walls,
the stone fountain
just like the one in Rome,
the dark red carpets
and candlelight dripping wax.
The waiters hovered about us
in dark corners watching
and waiting like vultures.
I remember the coat check,
the tiny tables,
low light, always the same
pasta. Mr. Bing always
ordered scallops and split pea
soup. He sent the soup back
if it was too hot or too cold.
For dessert he had a little hot
coffee with a lot of hot milk.
He carried a little card that
said *All I want is a little
hot coffee with a lot of hot milk.*
When the waiter came to remove
the plates, he would get out
this card. Then he would count
and recount his money.

"How much money
do I have?" he would ask.
He had millions,
but could never remember it.
"What time is it?" "Did I pay?"
When we returned to his penthouse apartment
on Central Park South, he would
check the closets for ghosts.
He died in January or December,
I believe. It was on the front
page of *The New York Times*,
his picture jumping out at me
like his face in bed.

EEG WITH BRANDY ALEXANDER

I am lying cold in a white bed
hooked up to a computerized machine
while it records my brain activity.
The technician says to stop rolling my
eye balls while my eyes are closed. "I'm not rolling
them!" I say. She tells me to "Shut up!"
"You're not allowed to talk during the procedure."
Then she begins to flash the multi-colored
strobe lights. She does this for five minutes.
"Some patients have seizures during this part,"
she says, hoping I will have one, so that
she can go to lunch. I hope I don't.
She makes a telephone call to a friend.
They chat while I am attached to the machine,
my brain recording its lines on the screen.

Maybe I'll get out alive.
Maybe she'll send a volt from the machine
that will travel up the wires pasted
into my head at the speed of light,
and I'll catch on fire. Maybe she'll have a
Brandy Alexander with a blue flame
to celebrate. "I can see
your eyeballs on the computer screen.
Are you drowsy yet?" The maid comes in
to shelve the fresh cotton
sheets for the next patient.
It's as though the flesh on my face
is being staked out for an incision.
What will the doormen say when I enter
in a scarf hiding the paste in my wet hair
with red marks on my forehead?

SEIZURE

My father always said that I never
got epilepsy from his side of the
family, the clocking ticking like a time
bomb in the dark hallway, and for a long
time I thought that some vengeful god
had knocked me in the head out of spite,
until one night lying in bed thinking
about it, I realized I knew
that I had inherited epilepsy from YOU,
—I never imagined it before because
you were always attacking me, the scape
goat, the unhealthy one—you were never
sick a day in your life—but then I remembered
your fall at the college and being trapped
under the wheel of the car, and the accident
in the dentist's office, and the time you
broke your leg in the yard for no reason,
and there were the unexplained seizures
in the Nursing Home—and I knew you had
the falling sickness all along and boasted
that you were never sick a day in your
life, never even saw a seizure before
mine, except the girl at Brenau College
in Georgia, and you couldn't look, you said,
while I loaded up on Dilantin
that made me fat and sluggish and caused my
gums to swell and my hair to fall out.
And there was the time you gave my brother
complete power of attorney over
your life (and mine because he was in charge
of my inheritance and spent it all)
by disinheriting me, a kind of
left-handed seizure, and you denied it all.

RECOVERY

The long gowns lie in my arms like dead lovers,
corpses that nestle against my shoulder and climb
down my back like vines clinging to a trellis.
Silent, they possess me and wrap themselves
around me like snakes resisting my touch as I
scoop them up, holding them against my face,

tawny straw honey flaxen-colored
silks and satins,
robes embroidered with pearls set in gold.

I labor, bending over
the evening clothes on the ground
to recover what is lost, picking them up,
like women tending rice paddies in a muddy field
a terrace of taffeta dresses, net and tulle
pink as a cloud of silk, a flooded field of evening wear.

BELL JAR

Got a queer and almost overpowering
urge to write today, or typewrite,
my whole novel on the pink stuff,
lovely textured Smith memorandum
pads of 100 sheets each:

a fetish somehow, seeing a
hunk of that pink paper,
different from all the endless
reams of white bond, my task seems
finite, special, rose-cast.

Bought a rose bulb for
the bedroom light today
and have already robbed enough
notebooks from the supply closet
to do one and a half drafts of
a 350 page novel
in rose-vermillion,

a dinner party scene,
vinously blurred, (letting) lamb
fat and blood congeal to pale grease
on the scattered plates,
wine sediment curd in the bottom
of glasses.

TO PHOENICIA

This is a three-hour trip.
I finish my Diet Pepsi and put
The empty can on the floor.
It begins to roll up and down the bus aisle.
There is a forty-minute layover in Kingston.
A man gets on the bus with another man, each with
A brown paper bag, and they sit behind me.
The men open their
Paper bags and begin to eat garlic chicken
Sandwiches. They smell up the bus. I can hear them
Chew the smelly chicken as we ride into
The mountains. Behind me, they
Talk about getting drunk and passing out.
I think of Rip Van Winkle and of how he
Drank too much whiskey and slept for thirty years
In a mountain hollow as the bus begins to move.
The can rolls to the other end of the bus,
Making a hollow clanging sound.
The highways are clothed in goldenrod.

Margaret Barbour Gilbert is an award-winning writer from Alabama who lives in New York City. She has published two chapbooks of poems with Finishing Line Press, *My Grandmother's Engagement Ring* and *Blue Electrode*. A play, *A Scene Of Captivity With Waltzes And Mirrors* has been staged twice at Harvard's Agassiz Theater. "Eating Oatmeal" from *My Grandmother's Engagement Ring* is included in the Alfred Knopf anthology, *Conversation Pieces: Poems That Talk To Other Poems*. She has been seizure-free since 1989.

www.ingramcontent.com/pod-product-compliance
Lightning Source LLC
LaVergne TN
LVHW041506070426
835507LV00012B/1356